The Pawn Queen
(The Making of the 21st Century Black Female)

The Pawn Queen
(The Making of the 21st Century Black Female)

Byron Woulard

Copyright 2010 Byron Woulard

ISBN 978-0-982-93751-8

Dedication

This book is dedicated to all the women and men that I have had the pleasure of learning something from

Introduction

This book was written because countless books have been written and numerous documentaries have been filmed over the years since Africa was invaded and colonized by the European man about the Black male and how we have been brainwashed, but no one has truly touched on the brainwashing of the Black female. Why this is, goes unsaid, but the time for this revealing is now and this is what this book is about.

I chose the title The Pawn Queen because it's a double entendre as it can be used for Chess or it can be a play of words eluding to the fact that Black women, whom have been called Black Queens, have been used as pawns to help bring about a certain result in the Black community, unbeknownst to the them. If you play Chess or are familiar with the game then you know that the pawn is the only piece that can take on the form of another piece on the board if it is advanced to the last row of the board and the queen is the most powerful piece on the board because it can move in any direction on the board for as many spaces it wants to. So in Chess a pawn can become a queen and in life a Queen can be used as a pawn.

As a Black male I know from experience when and where the Black male's mis-education began within my generation, Generation X, and as a wise man I have come to realize that this brainwashing wasn't directed at just us. The Black female has been subjected to the same methods as we were and she has been and still is falling victim to these manipulative ploys that were set into effect when we were slaves.

The problem with this is that she does not know that she has been brainwashed also. She thinks that everything about herself is what she wants it to be and nothing more. She does not know that the way she thinks about herself is a direct effect of a cause set into motion many years before she was born. My mother, grandmother, great grandmother and beyond were being mis-educated over the decades to eventually produce what we see today.

The Pawn Queen, the most effective weapon for the ultimate goal, the annihilation of the Black man and the Black family. I say Black man and not Black woman because the strength of a people lies within the strength of the man and so goes the man so goes the woman and so goes the family, thus leading to a destruction of the people. Destroying a people does not necessarily mean to eliminate them from existence. It can also mean making them feel as if nothing good can come from his race thus making him want to assimilate into other cultures and shun the very people who started civilization. As many philosophers have said throughout time, if you can condition the mind to think inferior, then that person will find their place and stay in it, you won't have to tell them what to do they'll just do it themselves. Can anyone deny that this is where we are as a people, that we have become our own worst enemies?

Surely some will read this and say that I am a Black woman basher, that I didn't receive love from my mother or that a Black woman scarred me, but if you read this and take it in with a open heart you will see that everything that I am saying in these pages are true. This is not true of all women just as the brainwashing of the Black male has not made all Black males gun toting drug dealing thugs, but it helped to create the African American Male Diaspora that we see within our society today. No one can deny this fact, it is truth, and if you deny the truth then you will never be free of the shackles of the mind.

For those who don't believe that the mind can be enslaved, drive through any inner city in America and then do the same in an inner city in another state. The scenes are identical. This is not by coincidence, it is by design. Did the ghetto youth design this environment, or was it somehow translated to them from another source. If it wasn't by their own design then who designed it for them and for what reason? And why do so many partake in what the ghetto has to offer as if it's the only thing they can do?

This has been the subject of countless studies and inquiries when the Black male is the control group, but who has done this study about the Black female. Why does the Black female think like she thinks, why does she act the way she acts?

I have learned over my years that asking questions lead to answers but asking the right questions lead to the truth. If you are not afraid of the truth then this book will surely guide you to a better understanding of who you are and why you are constantly at odds with the Black male and other Black females. It will lead you to a better understanding of self and will eventually set you free of the notion that there are no good Black males out there, or that Black men can't handle a strong Black woman or that Black men want women of other races.

Whatever your position in life may be this book will help you better understand the reasons behind why you think and behave the way you do and will give you the insight to communicate better with other women who have fallen victim to the same conditioning that you have. It will surely help you to see that the Black man isn't the only one who has been thoroughly brainwashed and made to think in a manner conducive to being a second class citizen on the come up in a first class (read white) world.

We are all in the same boat, let's stop fighting with one another and row in unison. We are all trying to reach the same destination. I have your back, I hope you have mine.

Contents

Introduction vii

Some One Please Call 911 (The Raping of the Slave
Woman A brief synopsis) 1

Light Skin Good Hair Favoritism 5

The Black Man White Woman Myth 9

I Have Good Hair Syndrome 11

Black Beauty As Defined by White Men 13

From Civil Rights to Hip Hop 15

Civil Rights 17

Affirmative Action and the Beginning of the Independent
Woman 19

Blaxploitation 23

Crack is Wack 25

The 80's Babies 27

Hip Hop (The Gift and the Curse) 29

In Steps Lil Kim 31

Stick (Trina takes the baton) 35

Stick (Nicki Minaj takes the baton) 39

The Rise of the Video Vixen 43

The Exotic Dancer 47

The Internet & Black Girls Gone Wild 51

The Mirror Model 53

And Along Came Superhead (The Karrine Steffans Phenomenon) 55

The Porn Star 57

Reality TV and the Nationalization of Black Female Stereotypes 61

Baller Alert (When Being a Groupie Becomes Option # 1) 67

From Now to Forever.. 71

The Conclusion 73

Some One Please Call 911
(The Raping of the Slave Woman A brief synopsis)

The raping of slave women by their masters was common place during the Trans-Atlantic slave trade. This is one of the main reasons we have so many lighter skinned Black Americans, but it was not done to create a "fairer" skinned offspring, it was done for more insidious reasons which I will attempt to break down to you for the purpose of framing this book so that you can see where the beginning of the utilization of the Black female as "The Pawn Queen" started.

The raping of the slave woman was done for a few reasons, notwithstanding the white man's lust for the beautiful African Goddess, which were to bring about a certain feeling within the woman, man and child. The overall feeling was to instill fear in the slaves to make them understand who was in charge and that revolt and uprisings would be met with brutal force and death, just as they do today. You can see it in all the wars, 10 to 20 times more people die than the amount of American lives that are lost.

For the male, the raping of the slave woman was done to make him feel helpless and unable to protect the women of his tribe, the way he would have been bound by tribal honor to defend them from attack from foreign invaders if they were back in their homeland. If the woman was his wife he would then have the feeling of helplessness coupled along with the fact that his wife had been with the very man or men that enslaved them. As a man in 2010, knowing that your wife has been with another man or men, even if she was raped, is a deeply disturbing fact that can translate into all kinds of problems, but at least we can do something about it, like divorce or therapy. During the years of slavery a man could literally do nothing except for try to come to grips with it or attack the master at which point he would be put to death. And because a person's basic instinct is survival, it meant that he would have to deal with knowing that he was powerless in a situation where his instincts as a man should have taken over and addressed the situation. After the rape and when she is back with him, he is now having every thought imaginable racing through his brain. Did she like it, does she want to do it again, etc, etc, etc. The day after the initial rape their entire world has changed and he is now forced to live in it. If she was considered "good in bed" then the master would frequent her often so imagine what that does to the thinking of the male. Now imagine if she becomes pregnant by the master and the baby is born interracial! He has to then live with this child of rape and still be a husband to her and a father to the child. These are but a few examples of what the Black male had to endure after the female was raped so you know that what she had to endure was much worst.

For the female slave who had to endure this heinous treatment, it had to create a psychological disaster within her mind, along with the physical pain associated with the act, the hell she had to experience had to be horrendous. To be sitting in your home and the very man who enslaved you kicks in the door and demands you to come with him. You don't know what he is about to do. Is he going to rape you, beat you, or kill you? As he grabs her she looks over at her father, brother, or husband with fear in her eyes and they can do nothing but sit there. Surely a lot of slaves in this situation died to protect the woman but it was in vain for the most part because if he didn't kill the master he would be tortured, castrated and then put to death. And the slave master would still end up raping the woman and in some cases putting her to death also, and even if he killed the slave master he would still end up murdered by the hands of the slave masters family or friends. So inevitably he was facing a lose, lose, lose situation, because nothing good could come out of it.

After this atrocious crime she is now taken back to the slave quarters and has to confront the men who let her get raped, although they would have been killed if they tried to intervene, it still had to be hard to reconcile that they did nothing.

If the slave master liked the slave woman then he would frequent her more often and begin to show her favoritism when she was around the other slaves. The slave woman who began her relationship as a rape victim would then rationalize that her aggressor was the only man that could save her or rescue her from slavery. In psychology this is akin to a kidnap victim actually sympathizing with the kidnapper or what is called the Stockholm syndrome. It's a mechanism that comes directly from the driving force of man, survival. If none of the male slaves could stop this from happening to her, the only way she can stop it is by becoming the willing participant of it. If she makes the slave master believe that she likes what they are doing and that she likes him he will eventually not allow any of the other men to touch her, his friends or any other slave either. Now she has security although it comes from the very man that made her feel insecure in the first place.

This type of behavior would create jealousy and envy amongst slave women who wanted to be treated better, especially in the younger ones who may not have known that her relationship with the slave master was born out of rape. They would then try to catch the eye of the slave master or one of his friends or male family members with the hope of being rescued somewhat from their dismal existence. Over time the slave master would not have to forcefully rape the slave women because they had willing participants who were seeking to be treated better.

This is not true of all slave women but a lot of them began to develop this thought pattern and it is manifesting itself today in our society in various ways in our Black women. The same conditioning principles at work then are being utilized today. They are making sure that the Black woman feels as if the Black man cannot protect her, provide for her or her children, and the only man that can is the white man. He can give her good jobs, good housing and treat her like the Queen she is. She can feel more secure with him than with a Black man, whom has been portrayed as the worst being on this planet through various media outlets since the dawn of media.

As this subject in itself can be the subject of countless pages I decided to make it as brief as possible, but gave you a synopsis of what the raping of slave women will do to a person's thinking, both woman and man. In the following chapters you will see where some of these thought patterns are still prevalent within our communities and you will see how the techniques of the slave masters were implemented after slavery to reacquaint us with the 260 or so years of actual brainwashing while we were slaves. You will see how this forced thinking became a part of who we are and now we think as if we are still the slave although we are free in body, we are now slaves in the mind.

Light Skin Good Hair Favoritism

This thought pattern was the direct result of the first interracial children being born to the raped slave woman during slavery. During slavery the interracial children that the slave master or his wife allowed to live were considered to be better looking than the children of two slave parents. The slave master would sometimes even allow the child to have better clothing, food, and an education. These were things expressly denied to the other dark skinned "bad hair" kids of the slaves.

As the interracial slave child grew older, as any child would have, she would recognize the difference in treatment as did the other slave children. The child of two slave parents would then be ridiculed and called names by the interracial kids because they would here these names being used by the master toward the full African slaves and their children but they would hardly ever if ever be hurled toward them. So in their psyche they deduced that the way they looked was good and the way the other slave looked was ugly. And we all know how real children can be.

This became a major problem in the female slave child because women are constantly in need of affirmation of their beauty by those who they love or those who love them. It's an archetypal thought that has developed throughout the ages as the most attractive women were the ones that the men of early tribes wanted as mates. Women have always been chosen as opposed to doing the choosing. So as this developed over time a female child would inherently have these same thoughts growing up. Then the father of said child would reinforce this thought by constantly telling her she is beautiful so as she gets older this is what she will come to expect from a man. The father did this so that she would have self worth and confidence in herself and her beauty. Without a father or father figure in her life a woman will search for a male that gives her confidence and assure her of her beauty.

The problem with the female slave child is based mostly on her interactions with the men of the plantation and the other children. As stated earlier the slave master used every tactic imaginable to break slaves and one of them was to make the female slave distrust the male slave and feel as if the male slave was more of a hindrance to her than a help. He, the slave master, made sure that she did not feel secure like she needed to feel with the male slave and he made sure that she believed that her appearance was ugly and unsightly although he still had sex with her. He was not in the business of building her up he was in the business of tearing her down so that he became her everything.

This mind state was passed down from mother to daughter over time and it became a part of their survival mechanism and the most basic instinct of all human beings is survival, so anything that seemed to position someone in a better position for survival would quickly be a trait adopted by the rest of the slaves. In this instance it would be the acceptance of the slave masters views of beauty and self worth. With her self-worth directly tied to the very man that held not only her life but the quality of her life as well in balance it would behoove her to think as he wanted her to think.

This meant complimenting the white women of the plantation on their beauty and elegance all while in front of the female slave child. The slave child would hear this and come to the realization that white women were all beautiful and elegant. As psychiatrists have learned since then and what everyone knows now is that children mimic action more than they do what they are told to do. What this is saying is that, if a child sees and hears you complimenting white women all the time then they will come to believe that what they see is true. You can say to them afterword, "I'm just saying that to make them feel good" but that would be a double edged sword because when you say it to them later on they will question why you said it. And as I grew up and I know as the vast majority of us 30 something's grew up, we all can attest to our parents not explaining anything to us. The key phrase after you ask a lot of questions was "because I said so or don't worry about that."

This is the same attitude that they were taught by their mothers and their mothers were taught by their mothers and so on. So as you can see if the wrong reasoning was adopted during slavery and it passed on to their children who then passed it on to their children, you can see how we end up where we are today.

The beauty of the Black female was dictated by the slave master. The slave woman adopted this thought pattern because it was conducive to her survival thus it became part of her psyche and then she passed it down to her child.

As the female slave child grew older and was being conditioned by her mother, father, friends, slave masters and observation, the only logical conclusion would be the one that the female slave still carries until this day. The interracial slave was treated better than the regular slaves, the white woman with her long flowing hair was considered elegant and beautiful, the regular slave was called ugly and ridiculed by the slave master and the interracial slave children. So her only mechanism for survival would be to accept this condition as true and long to get out of it. If she did not except it then she would always be in conflict with the others around her and that would make for an unhappy life.

As she internalized her condition it became part of a psychological defect that would manifest itself later on as the Black woman of the late 1800's and early 1900's. The one that adopted the hair care products that could straighten their hair like the beautiful elegant white women so that they could be more acceptable. It would become the I Have Good Hair Syndrome that women manifest today.

Also during the post slavery era between the late 1800's and early 1900's the lighter skinned Blacks tried to segregate themselves from the darker skinned Blacks by implementing what was called "the brown paper bag test". This test was done to keep Blacks who were darker than a paper lunch bag out of certain groups and fraternities. The comb test and the blue vein test were commonly practiced during this period also.

So as soon as we were freed you can see the psychological effect of the slave masters conditioning being utilized by light skinned Blacks on dark skinned Blacks. So at this point you had two groups of people whom were the same people that ridiculed being dark and "ugly" during slavery now creating cast systems after slavery. The Black woman had to be light skinned and have good hair so that she can be perceived as beautiful but now it was coming for the Black man and woman also.

What does this do to the thinking of Black women? The darker skinned ones wanted to be lighter and lighter ones thought they were better than the darker ones. And it seemed to be corroborated by the coming of the Black man white woman myth that white men started during slavery that gave rise to Black men being lynched throughout the south.

The Black Man White Woman Myth

During this same period after slavery the white man was afraid that all the atrocious things that he did to the Black woman, the now free Black man would do to the white woman. During slavery the white man would often refer to a strong well hung slave as a breeder, the same as they did with horses and other live stock that exuded masculinity, and part of his fear was always that the white woman would want to be with slaves because of them being considered as sexual gods due to the fact that they were well endowed and masculine.

After slavery had ended and the Black man was free to roam about and in an effort to keep white women from trying to experience the sexual prowess of the Black man, they would try to make white women afraid of Black men by saying that he wanted to rape them and do harm to them because he used to be a slaves and they were angry. Some of them believed it and if they felt like a slave looked at them wrong they would tell their husbands or the police and this is when lynching began to rise in the US.

Black men would be strung from trees for just speaking to a white woman. Emmitt Till was one of the most known cases of this, although he wasn't lynched in the conventional sense, when a white woman thought he was whistling at her she became afraid thus setting off the insanity of white men which resulted in them murdering him at the age of 14, and this was in 1955. What they fail to tell you about this era and it had to be told by Black historians is that the vast majority of lynching's were preceded by castrations. The castrations were a direct message for all to see. If you think you're going to have sex with our women think again, we'll kill you first.

During this era Black women were repeatedly told that Black men wanted these women because they were the forbidden fruit. Surely some Black men wanted them but the psyche of the Black woman up to that point had been conditioned to think that white skin and straight hair was beautiful, thus all things white was what Black men wanted. It didn't help when one of the most notable Black men of that era, a boxer by the name of Jack Johnson would be seen gallivanting around with white women. This helped to reinforce the condition within Black women and helped lead to the I Have Good Hair Syndrome.

I Have Good Hair Syndrome

When people start talking about the subject of "good hair" Madam CJ Walkers name is always the first to come up. This is because she is widely held as being the inventor of the perm and/or straightening comb, which is not true. She was considered to be the first woman to become a millionaire by her own efforts without marrying into it or through inheritance, but the perm and straightening comb came into existence by white men who utilized them for the exact opposite of what we use them for.

Karl Nessler, a German barber invented the perm in the late 1800's or early 1900's and a Frenchman by the name of Marcel Grateau invented the curling iron/straightening comb circa 1872. Historically speaking white women wanted to have curly hair because they felt like having curly hair instead of straight hair was more attractive so they would try different ways to get their hair to be curly and stay that way.

Later down the line Madam CJ Walker invented products to help baldness and to maintain and grow black hair. She opened up schools and taught these already invented methods to her students, thus popularizing them within the black community. This was the beginning of the Black hair care industry as we see it today and that's what made her a millionaire.

So as white women were trying to achieve a curly ethnic look black women were trying to achieve the exact opposite by straightening their hair. This was done because they felt that black men coveted white women, so in order to stay competitive with their white counterpart they had to at least have comparable hair as she did, as the vast majority of black women of those times were of a darker skin tone the only thing that they could do to appear more like her white counterpart was to have straight hair. The lighter skinned black women who were the products of interracial mixing would usually have curly hair, so they to fell victim to straightening their hair also so that they could look closer to being white. This created two advantages for them because they could either become more desirable amongst black men or they could possibly pass as being white and then marry a white man.

Black Beauty
As Defined by White Men

Then in the 1920's along came Josephine Baker, I light skinned black woman who became known as one of the most beautiful women alive. She rose to fame as a chorus girl doing vaudeville shows and later opened in Paris where she became an international star, because she was willing to appear almost completely nude, which landed her in silent movies, thus showing the world the lighter skinned straight haired black woman was to be revered as a sex symbol.

Then along came Lena Horne, Dorothy Dandridge and Eartha Kitt, to name a few of the noticeable ones of the early to mid 1900's. All these women were and still are revered as sex symbols in the eyes of blacks and whites alike. Of these four women all but one had white and Native American mixed blood, that one being Dorothy, but what she had in common with the others was her light skin and "good hair". These were the women that other women of their time viewed as role models and as beautiful because they were stars and were considered by every man even white men as such. Once again the black woman is being confronted with the perception that beauty is something other than what the vast majority of them looked like back then, thus continuing the conditioning that has gotten us to where we are today.

The culmination of this era which began during slavery up to the civil rights era saw the Black woman be reduced to a sexual toy for white men, she was conditioned to believe that the slave master was her savoir and the key to her survival. She was also conditioned to believe that all things pertaining to white women were beautiful and that Black skin and kinky hair was ugly and disgusting. Then she was conditioned to believe that Black men wanted white women thus making her believe that the only way she could get a Black man was to become as close to her white counterpart as possible. This could be done by bleaching creams and straightening the hair during the first 50 years after slavery. Although she was free from the chains of slavery she had no idea that she was now been shackled in her mind and that a lot of what she thought about herself and Black men was the direct result of conditioning that the slave master used to keep her, the Black man and child in check.

Then came the women's liberation movements and civil rights which saw a new form of conditioning become the way to keep these new found attitudes from unleashing the Black female from her mental bondage. The methods stayed the same but the tools used would change due to the ever evolving landscape of this new era.

TV, radio and movies were the new way to disseminate information to the masses and the message to the Black woman was to keep her thinking the way she thought during slavery and directly after slavery.

From Civil Rights to Hip Hop

Between the Jim Crow Era and the Civil Rights Era the Black woman had been pretty much marginalized to a help mate for the Black man. Although a few, like Madam CJ Walker had risen to prominence through hard work and ingenuity, the others that became nationally known were singers and actresses. Women like Josephine Baker, Lena Horne, Dorothy Dandridge, and Eartha Kitt had become internationally known for their entertainment value and were treated like sex symbols. These women were of fair skin and wore their hair straight like white women. Although most Black women didn't fit this mold at that time more and more were trying to because of the programming and conditioning of the slave master.

As you've read, Black women and men started to create groups and organizations that utilized old slave practices to grant membership. The "brown paper bag test, the blue vein test and the comb test were widely used by these organizations to either, admit or deny membership into these societies. This in turn gave rise to a Black elitist community whose sole purpose was to keep the light skinned, good hair Black community separate from the average Black person. Because this community had been shown favoritism by the slave master during and directly after slavery it was a well educated and affluent community. So naturally Black women who were of a darker skin tone wanted to fit in and achieve the status of the Dorothy Dandridge's and affluent Black women of their time, so they were quicker to adopt new methods of achieving these dreams. They never knew that the way they were thinking about each other would become the next phase of worldwide racism that is now coming to be known as Colorism, where the darker skinned people of every race would be discriminated against.

Darker skinned women didn't make it into the mainstream as sex symbols until the 50's and 60's but by then the damage was done. There were literally millions of women trying to achieve this white standard of beauty and even with the civil rights and black is beautiful movements that encompassed the 50's, 60's and 70's our sisters were still lost in this paradoxical self defeating thought pattern, but they didn't realize it, they thought it was just what they wanted to do or how they wanted to act. They had no clue that they were being conditioned the same way the Black man was being conditioned to be a mental slave. We still see remnants of this conditioning in our women today, with them wanting to be with the light skinned man or the one with "good hair" so that their baby will come out light skinned with "good hair", or you hear the ever so popular phrase, "I have Indian in my family".

This all started in the late 1800's and continues on into modern times. Spike Lee even touched on it in his highly acclaimed movie School Daze, released in 1988. So now it's 2010 and the real reason why black women started perming and straightening their hair has been lost to a hundred years of denial and conditioning.

Civil Rights

As Civil Rights was getting started in the 1950's Black women had already had roughly 350 years of conditioning to make them think a certain way about themselves and the Black man. Light skinned was better than dark skin, straight hair was better than kinky hair and the white man was better for her than the Black man. But the rise of Martin Luther King Jr and Malcolm X along with Black pride started to put a dent in the conditioning of the slave master.

Black women were witnessing a re-birth of the strong Black man persona, the one that was willing to die for what he believed in, as opposed to the slave that was obedient to the status quo and took what the master gave him. This new found Black pride was what she had been searching for since our capture and subsequent enslavement by the white man. It seemed like we were on our way towards equality and strength as Black people in this nation. The Black king had come back, so the Black queen was starting to resurface also.

Then something happened. The Civil Rights movement began to be defined by those who opposed it and the things that we were fighting for lead us back to the very thing that we were trying to get away from in the first place, the white man. The movement became a movement of integration into the white community because we thought that everything white was better than everything Black.

Before the Civil Rights Movement we had to take care of each other and create business' that catered to Black people because white people didn't want us in their establishments. We owned our destinies and then we gave it up to become "equal" to whites. Once again we were basing all things good off what white people thought was good. This was a great era for Black people in general but overtime we would start to see how this era would unfold to shape us going into the 21st century.

This was a great time for Black women also, as it spawned women like Rosa Parks, Angela Davis, Maya Angelou, Tina Turner, Diana Ross, Nichelle Nichols of Star Trek fame, Pam Grier, Jayne Kennedy, Lola Folana, Nina Simone and so on. These women were all notable women of their day and all but 3 of them were singers or actresses.

And since this era which ones have you heard the most about? We only talk about Rosa Parks during Black History Month, Angela Davis is only spoken of in Black Power circles and Maya Angelou see's a little bit of shine whenever they need a poem spoken and Nina Simone only gets mentioned when talking about Jazz or the Blues, but Pam Grier, Tina Turner and Diana Ross are still being spoken of today in many circles.

Why is this? Because they were the ones that the new Black woman had to pattern themselves after in order for the brainwashing to continue. You can't condition the mind to stay a mental slave by feeding it revolutionary thought. In order to get the desired response from 100's of years of conditioning and get the ball back on track they had to give the Black female the image that they wanted her to pursue. And that image was that of the singer and the actress. And as Black women pursued their dreams other things were unfolding that would have greater ramifications on the future than they could have imagined.

Affirmative Action and the Beginning of the Independent Woman

Affirmative Action was a system put into place by the government in the 60's to help level the playing field for Blacks after the Civil Rights Movement had demanded equal opportunity for Black citizens. Affirmative Action by no means was a bad thing but going into the 80's corporations that didn't want to come off as racist and insensitive to the Black plight found a small loop hole. This loop hole was that AA was not just meant for people of color as the constitution prohibits any laws that directly target any racial group. It had to read minorities in the work place, not Blacks in the work place. The loophole that had been discovered was that women were considered a minority in the workplace also. At the time this law was enacted white women had been fighting for equality amongst the genders also under what is now considered the second wave of the Women's Lib Movement. When the AA laws were put on the books and it became inevitable that Black people and women were going to get their fair share of jobs it only took a little while for the status quo CEO to realize that Black women were a double minority.

Now instead of hiring two people, a Black man and a white woman they could just hire one person, a Black woman and because it's in the best interest of white people he could still hire a white woman if two positions needed to be filled. During the late 70's and early 80's just about every factory job that didn't need heavy lifting was now being filled by Black and white women.

Since the enacting of AA laws the black woman has steadily risen in the workplace and has since become larger in numbers than the Black male. To date there are more Black women in the workforce than Black men and more Black women in supervisorial rolls or higher positions, and we are the only race in America with these statistics. This was the direct result of AA laws and the coming crack cocaine epidemic that saw 100's of thousands to millions of Black men becoming drug dealers, inmates and becoming exempt from the workforce due to criminal records.

I am in no way trying to diminish the accomplishments of Black women in the workplace but this has to be spoken of in context with everything else so that the bigger picture can become more apparent and easier to see. Black women did what they needed to do to keep the Black community from falling into the abyss and I commend them for it but with the rise of the Black woman in the workforce came a new self sufficient attitude. A lot of these Black women started working to help their husbands/men with the bills because they wanted a better existence for their children, but some were forced to get jobs out of necessity because the father of the child was not around to provide for her or her child. And because they were strong enough to hold down the family in their time of need they begin to adopt a new thought pattern that helped create the independent woman dogma that we see and hear today through various forms of media.

Some of the Black women who were forced into the workforce because of the absentee father grew bitter toward men and began to pass on this bitterness and anger to their children. As they were championing themselves as great parents because they were able to stave off poverty by becoming a career minded Black woman they were constantly belittling the Black man by talking down on him and painting a picture of a deadbeat in the their children's minds. These newly independent women were quick to demean a man but would always have a new man when they got rid of their old man.

The daughters of these women were the ones who were quick to adopt the independent woman attitude and believe that she did not need a man, although she would constantly be looking for a man just like her mother.

Now in 2010 we see Black women that believe that they don't need a man when they can provide things for themselves. So what this is saying is that the only reason a woman needs a man is to provide things for her and if she can do it for herself she doesn't need a man. This is the attitude of the independent woman that we see so often being spewed as what being independent is all about. This is why so many Black women rebel against the statement of "know your role". They believe that the role of the Black woman within the household has changed due to so many women having to hold down the house because of absentee fathers.

The major problem with this thought pattern is that when they find a man that can and will hold down the family they don't know how to turn the independent woman attitude off. Now when they get into arguments they try to belittle the man in his efforts. And if the Black woman makes more money than the Black man it gets even worse as if everything in a relationship boils down to whose paycheck is the biggest. Men have no problem with making more than women, but most Black women when entering a relationship with a Black man have a problem with it.

They act as if they should be deemed the head of the household because their paychecks are larger and this is what they usually base their independence off of, the ability to make more than their male counterpart, which is far from what true independence is. So what started out as a means for survival became an attitude that is now becoming a wedge between Black men and women in America that is destroying our relationships.

Blaxploitation

As affirmative action was kicking in and trying to level the playing field for Blacks in general, some Black women were starting to feel the pain of raising children on their own as the dead beat dad era was staring to become part of the Black mentality across the nation. Black men were leaving their families and leaving the Black woman to fend for herself in his pursuit of Superfly-ness and trying to be the Mack. These women would be the ones that ended up on Public AIDS and fell victim to the coming crack epidemic, which in turn helped create the Lil Kim Syndrome. I call it Public AIDS because it weakened the Black family and caused us to fall into a disease like state of dependency on the government for handouts. In itself it was an admirable thing because it helped to keep people from starving to death but as the 80's came around it had started to become the bane of our existence. They also were the ones that gave rise to the Lil Kim Syndrome and ushered in the use what you got to get what you want era.

As Black people were just coming out of the Civil Rights Era we were flush with feelings of accomplishment and were trying to forge new roads for ourselves. At the same time the new militant movement was starting to become more main stream because of the assassination of MLK Jr and the powers that be were was not about to let their hard work over the decades go to waste so the Blaxploitation era was born.

Pam Grier, the original Foxy Brown debuted in films in the 70's, was best known for her roles in Coffy and Foxy Brown where she was the a gun wielding vigilante that was out for justice. She would do whatever it took to get her revenge even if it meant becoming a prostitute to infiltrate an organization and destroy it from the inside. She got her start in earlier women in prison exploitation films where she pretty much played the same role and demonstrated that if she had to take her clothes off for a role she was ok with it. This was the image that a lot of Black women looked upon as empowering. She wore the hip afro and the sexy garb of the 70's and she wore it well.

This era saw the likes of the Black woman being objectified and basically treated like shit, until Pam Grier entered the scene and showed Black women what they could do if they just put their minds to it. She was a folk hero for inner city downtrodden Black women and a large number of disenfranchised young Black women who had no fathers in their lives and a mother who loathed Black men. These women wanted to be like Foxy Brown and Coffy, they were in her predicament and if she could do it so could they. They thought it was that easy to get off of drugs and be the strong independent Black woman the way Foxy did in her movies but they were mistaken.

Crack is Wack

After the Blaxploitation era had shown Black women that they were powerful enough to get on drugs and back off of them with no problem, then came the crack epidemic. When crack cocaine hit the streets in the early 80's the epidemic grew so fast that we didn't know what hit us. Countless Black women became hooked on the drug either from their men or from being in destitute and searching for a way out of their abysmal situations.

Because crack was so addictive it only took one hit to become what we called a crack head. When this monster was let loose and Black women fell victim to it, it started a trend of mothers who didn't care about their kid's well being anymore. They were busy trying to chase down the next high and if that meant their kids would have to be at home alone then so be it. If they had to take the last money in the house for food and give it to the drug dealer for crack, then that was what they were doing. And when the money ran out but the high was still calling them, they sold whatever they could to get enough money for a hit of that rock, including sex. These were the ones that became full blown crack heads. Out all night, kids at home alone fending for themselves and when she was at home she would have men running in and out of the house exchanging sex for crack. Her kids saw and heard what no kid should ever have to see or hear on a daily basis.

What does this do to the psyche of a female child? Moms down and out selling sex for money and that's the only way they seem to be surviving. A child see's no wrong in their parents while growing up, what she says and does is going to be what that child patterns herself behind. The child doesn't look at the crack as the monster in the room that's destroying their lives they just know that their lives aren't that good and the one constant is the line of men streaming in and out of the house who seem to help the situation because after they leave you can now afford groceries and the rent. The child doesn't understand that her mother is using the money she receives from public AID's, which should go toward food, clothing and shelter to feed her habit. It takes some years for a child to figure out why they are in the position that they are in and by that time they have more than likely fell victim to the neglect and wrong teachings of their mothers. By the time they have figured it out they too have turned into a revolving door for men and they are still in their early teens. This is what played out all over the ghettos of Black America. Just about any young male that grew up during this era knew which chicks were home alone and giving up the goodies while their mothers were out chasing a crack high.

These young Black teenage women who grew up during the crack era were the ones who would usher in the teenage pregnancy era and their kids, the 80's babies were the ones who propped up Lil Kim as a hero and role model for Black women.

The 80's Babies

The 80's babies who were being born to neglected teens and crack heads alike were coming into their tween and teen years right when Hip Hop was taking off as the driving force behind Black commerce and we saw it as the savior for Black people. The money that it was generating was astronomical so of course when older Black people put it down and railed against it, we thought they were crazy. How could you see something as big and beautiful as hip hop as a problem?

We couldn't even fathom it as being a curse in any way shape or form. How could something that is generating so much money and creating jobs for so many people be wrong? Because hindsight is 20/20 now I know what they were talking about. We were young and blinded by the big lights and money. We didn't even notice that the powers that be were using it to shape who we were, and who we thought we were, and what we thought we could become. We were angry and we finally had a medium that could showcase this anger and still get paid in the process, you couldn't beat that.

Crack was part of the landscape and hip hop was becoming the driving force for a Black economical base and we loved it. Black men were getting paid off crack and now we were getting paid off hip hop, which during the 80's was mostly positive and about partying and dancing. Some artist rapped about the harsh realities of the ghetto and they were rising steadily until NWA and The Geto Boys arrived on the scene and hip hop would be transformed forever and so would the Black woman.

As the Black female children of the crack era were becoming teenagers and moving into the formative years of their lives the driving force in Black communities were crack and Hip Hop. For the disenfranchised Black female who was searching for a way out of her situation a champion was on the horizon.

As we know, your teenage years are your most rebellious years, and for Back women who were lost, the drug dealer became her answer. He was able to provide for her the things that she wanted and thought that she needed in order to be happy and live a fulfilling life. Not only did they mess with drug dealers but a lot of their mother's and/or older sisters did it also, so it was always viewed as a viable way of obtaining stability and the finer things in life. But along with being with him came consequences that would help to shape her for many years to come.

As the teenage rebellion was taking place in Black girls across the nation and their psyche was being conditioned to feel and think in a certain manner Hip Hop birthed the champion of their generation and she would go one to create what I call the Lil Kim Syndrome.

Hip Hop (The Gift and the Curse)

To better understand how hip hop effected Black women, you must understand how it affected Black men first, as hip hop was a male dominated music genre for some time before women started to become emcees.

As a Black male I can remember when Ice Cube did a commercial for St Ides malt liquor. At the time, in the early to mid 90's 40 ounces of malt liquor were all the rage in the ghetto. Black re-activist were entrenched in verbal battles with TV cameras about how destructive this type of beer was, but as young Black men we didn't give a crap about what they were saying because we thought we knew everything. So we continued to drink it as long as they were selling it. Before the Ice Cube commercial, the malt liquor of choice in the hood was Olde English 800. We couldn't get enough of it, and then all of a sudden here comes Ice Cube, on TV doing a commercial about St Ides. Part of his lyrics verbatim was,"don't drink Olde English cause St Ides is given ends".

This was in reference to the fact that St Ides had paid Ice Cube to endorse its malt liquor and Olde English wasn't spending money with "Black people". At this point in hip hop emcees were not being paid to endorse products unless they were made by urban companies.

As an emcee that was a household name in the ghetto, and thought to be at that time a real thug, his words carried weight. It wasn't until his career was almost over that people came to realize that his whole persona was made up. It's what we call a studio gangsters now, but what we believed back then was that he was "real" and that was what we were searching for. So his words echoed beyond that commercial into real life and within a month of him singing the praise of St Ides, the company soared in its sells to urban youth, eventually overtaking Olde E in market share in the hood.

This phenomenon was repeated by Philly Blunts when an emcee made a rap called "How To Roll a Blunt". Marithe & Francois Girbaud, Versace, Tommy Hillfiger, Timberland, Crystal, and numerous other products have been rapped about by hip hop luminaries over the 30 year history of hip hop and guess what, they all saw a significant increase in profitability after rappers mentioned their products in songs. This was the beginning of the brainwashing through hip hop that gave rise to the Lil Kim Syndrome in Black women.

Here's the thing, if hip hop lyrics can get someone to spend their hard earned money on certain products without ever asking you to, except for Ice Cube's commercial, what do you think they can do to the thought pattern if they don't ask you to do anything? Since that first rhyme about a product I have seen firsthand how any product mentioned in a popular emcee's lyrics will go from good to great or from never heard of to the next hot thing. Jay Z knows about this firsthand because he stopped mentioning a certain Champaign brand after they refused to pay him to endorse there brand, but by the time he came to the realization that he needed to get paid for his endless rhymes about how great there product was it had become a household name and was seen in every refrigerator on MTV Cribs.

These are but a few examples of how hip hop was utilized as a marketing weapon in the inner cities of America. Now let us take a look at how hip hop was used as a carrier of subliminal messages to women.

In Steps Lil Kim

BLK (Before Lil Kim) women in hip hop were uplifting the Black female with their lyrics. Most of the female emcees BLK were women of distinction and were a part of the Black power hip hop movements of the 80's. You had women like Mc Lyte, Queen Latifah, Ms Melody, Salt and Pepa, Yo Yo, Monie Luv, etc. If you're old enough to remember these women, if not google them, you will quickly realize that most of them were not sexy, half naked femcee's but were for the most part, save one or two of them, overweight and wearing full garb. Salt and Pepa were the only ones out of this group of women who wore tight outfits but that was during the spandex era, which by the way is upon us again. But at least these women wrote lyrics about being respectful women

    ALK (After Lil Kim) you will see that the vast majority of female emcees that were allowed to grace the stage as nationally respected women emcees had to fit the Lil Kim mold.

    Hip hop had been usurped by the half naked gold digging hussy, as mom's used to call them. Lil Kim ushered in an entirely new brand of hip hop for women. She was a firebrand, she knew exactly what she wanted and it was money, sex, and partying. Her lyrics were brazen and unapologetic for who she was. No endearing moments of motherhood, no uplifting lyrics of the Black Queen, she was by her own words, the Queen Bee-itch. But what she did have was the attitude of the independent woman who doesn't know what being independent really is. She is the direct product of the use what you got to get what you want mind state that some black women teach their daughters. She was trying to escape her own reality by either getting a man with money or doing whatever it took to make money, as she willfully rapped about in her lyrics. For the most part she would write her own lyrics and Biggie would make sure that the words flowed properly to the beats and add his input to make sure she sounded good on her albums.

She was having sex with guys for money, being caught up in internet scandals of being rushed to the hospital and having cups, yes I said it cups of sperm siphoned from her belly, and various other scandals that for her improved her record sales, but would have sent a female emcee before her time to the poor house. But Lil Kim was resilient; her record sales soared and spawned many more wannabes and copy cats, i.e. Foxy Brown, etc.

In 1995 this was the image of Black women being distributed via the hip hop medium on video channels around the globe. Lil Kim, The Queen Bee-itch whose poster with her squatting down wearing a leopard skin lingerie outfit with her legs wide open became the poster of choice for Black boys and girls alike, was now the top femcee in hip hop. She was outselling a lot of the men so naturally she became an icon. Black girls whose parents allowed them to listen to Lil Kim were heavily influenced by her lyrics the same way Black boys were influenced by the lyrics of NWA and the other rappers who became household names during the early to mid 90's, which by the way saw a heavy spike in drug and gang related crimes across the nation. This was the new image for the Black female who didn't care about love and marriage as long as they were getting what they wanted, or so they said.

So let's put this in perspective, the image of the Black woman that was going to get hers no matter what she had to do to get it is now the number 1 image being disseminated throughout the world and being beamed into the homes of millions of disenfranchised angry young Black women. Women who are angry because their mothers were angry. Black mothers who were angry because the Black man left them for another Black woman or for a woman of another race who were spewing hateful venom toward the Black man whenever they got a chance. These angry mothers were the ones who allowed their daughters to listen to The Queen Bee-itch and eventually imitate her.

To help to reinforce the Lil Kim attitude in young Black women they had to elevate other female emcee's of her kind into the spotlight. Lauryn Hill was not a threat to this new mental state because she was part of a group and she didn't really come to the light of young Black women until The Fugees released The score in 96, by then Lil Kim had been followed by Foxy Brown, another scantily clad female emcee who boasted about her "use what you got to get what you want" persona.

Foxy Brown was more of the same, she was introduced as the Ill Na Na, which was a reference to her vaginal prowess. She was quickly positioned on every hip hop magazine out during that time wearing small slithers of clothing promoting the new image of the Black female to the masses. The age of the overweight female emcee rapping about something of substance was officially dead, except for Missy Elliot, but she rapped about the same things as Lil Kim and Foxy Brown did.

After Lil Kim came the likes of Eve, sexy, but her lyrics weren't as raunchy as her predecessors. She was an ex-stripper turned femcee and she enjoyed some years of fame that eventually spawned her a TV series.

From 1995 to 2000 you saw a myriad of female emcee's being paraded in front of the cameras as the "first lady" of every record company on the planet. There were a lot of misses during this period that faded into obscurity without ever making a solo album but one who came into the spotlight by a southern emcee named Trick Daddy was able to make a name for herself just as Lil Kim, Foxy Brown, Eve, and Missy Elliot did, and her name was Trina, "The Baddest Bitch".

Stick (Trina takes the baton)

"The Baddest Bitch" is the name she affectionately called herself and she would usher in some of the most graphic lyrics produced by a woman which gave rise to a host of copy cats who seemed to be trying to one up each other on sexually explicit lyrics just as male emcees would do to ascend to the top position of the industry. The only difference with the men when they started to get mass marketing was their lyrics were violent as opposed to sexual.

As for Trina I remember the lines that would change women in hip hop forever. It came on her debut song with Trick Daddy, Nann Nigga. In her verse she would say verbatim as found on metrolyrics.com;

> "You don't know nann **hoe** uh-uh
>
> Don' been the places I been
>
> Who can spend the grands that I spend
>
> **Fuck bout 5 or 6 best friends**
>
> And you don't know nann hoe uh-uh
>
> That's off the chain like me

That'll floss the thang like me

On a awful thang like me

You don't know nann **hoe** uh-uh

That sell more ass than me

You know nann **hoe**

That'll make you come like me

Nigga you don't know nann **hoe** uh-uh

That don' tried all types of shit

Who quick to deep throat the dick

And let another bitch straight lick the clit

Now you don't know nann **hoe** uh-uh

That'll keep it wet like me

Make it come back to back like me

Lick a nigga nut sack like me

Now you don't know nann **hoe** uh-uh

That'll ride the dick on the dime

Who love to fuck all the time

One who's pussy fatter than mine

Bitch you don't know nann **hoe**"

    The reason why I was able to pinpoint this as a major turning point in hip hop for females is because at the time I was interning at Red Distribution and had to listen to Trick Daddy's song over and over because I had to count out how many times the word nann was used in the song. Although Lil Kim talked about fellatio and vaguely referenced bi-sexuality in her lyrics she still had more than just sexual content in them. This was the first song that I could remember; I have to confess that I am not a fan of most female emcees spawned after Lil Kim arrived on the scene, including her. I listen to them on the radio but as for purchasing one there albums, it's not happening. So half of the stuff that they said on their explicitly labeled unedited albums I had not heard until I decided to write this book, but rest assured I've done the research for this chapter by simply asking the women who listen to these femcee's, and searching for their lyrics online.

As you can see by the snippets there was an escalation of sexually graphic lyrics from Lil Kim to Trina. And as you will see that these lyrics is now what's prominent in the rhymes of almost all of the female emcees who have some notoriety in the game today. Don't get me wrong, there are lots a female emcee's that don't rap about these things in their rhymes but they do not get national airplay if any airplay at all.

Why is this? Is this part of a plan or is it just how things shaped up? I'll comment on that later but back to hip hop ALK.

After Trina's triumphant burst onto the scene there were many women who tried to pattern themselves after her. Some patterned themselves behind Eve but never reached the fame that Eve reached. Femcee's like Rah Digga, Remy Ma and Shawna were sexy but had a little bit more to their styles than just plain old sexually charged bravado in their lyrics.

Others tried to directly imitate Trina and were sewn into the fabric of the Lil Kim femcee movement. Between Jackie O and Khia you would have thought that these women were ex-porn stars or something. And this is the trend that we see from around Trina's debut until now in 2010.

Stick (Nicki Minaj takes the baton)

2007 marked the beginning of the Nicki Minaj era. She has been massed marketed by the industry as the next great thing. From internet fame to worldwide fame via Young Money. The only female emcee in the group with sexually charged lyrics and a do or die attitude. Regarded as a lesbian up until she got with Young Money, now she is the number 1 female in hip hop. She has said in interviews that her inspirations were Lil Kim, Foxy Brown, Trina etc.

Surely we can all say, well those are some the top female emcees in the history of hip hop, but there are plenty other female emcees that she could have patterned herself behind that didn't bring a message of "use what you got to get what you want" to the ears of countless little girls across this nation. Nicki Minaj is the solidification of the Lil Kim era.

I believe that since the mass marketing of Lil Kim there has been a plan to systematically create the kind of Black women that we see today through hip hop. This is not indicative of all Black women but there is a very large amount of Black women who think with this attitude and wonder why they are in the positions that they are in today and they wonder why men treat them the way that they do.

Take a look at sexuality within the past 15 years, since the rise of the Lil Kim attitude. Black women are having way more sexual partners than any previous generation. When I was young you might have had a handful of women who had 5 to 10 sexual partners. In 2010 it's the norm and women are hitting these numbers at a much earlier age than before. Oral sex is not even an afterthought anymore. Over the past two generations Black women have embraced all things sexual with all of their sex partners. Nothing is reserved anymore for a long term relationship or marriage, and anyone reading this can attest to that.

Lil Kim was used to bring about a sexual revolution in Black women during a time when AIDS was on the rise in Black communities the world over and today what do we see, Black women are the number one group of women of women being infected with HIV and AIDS. This is not by coincidence, it's by design, and all you have to do is be truthful to yourself and you will see it.

This is not to say that Lil Kim was the sole reason for this, there were other factors that played into what we see today, such as the way Black men portrayed black women in videos and the way they degrade them in their songs since the rise of NWA, The 2 Live Crew and Too Short in the early 90's. All of these things had a part to play in the attitude of Black women today including their mothers and fathers, if they had a father in their lives. The lack of a father figure in the lives of Black females manifested itself within our communities as the Lil Kim Syndrome. This also gave rise to the stripper industry of the south that has created literally hundreds of thousands to millions of strippers across the nation trying to "survive". This will be discussed at length in another chapter, but because of the stripper we now have every woman with a web cam and computer trying to show off their striper moves on the internet.

Due to all these factors coming into play the only way to address the coming problems is to break them all down and find solutions to each and every one of them, but if we don't act now The Nicki Minaj era is going to see the Black female become little Nicki Minaj's and by any measure that is not good. It's not good for the Black male and female relationship and marriage percentage which makes it bad for the Black family.

Single mothers who continue to allow the Lil Kim Syndrome or the "use what you got to get what you want" attitude to be prevalent in their daughters will soon wake up to a Black marriage rate of 10% and a Black stripper rate of 90%. We can at least slow it down and eventually stop the attitude from prevailing if we take the time to admit that a lot of the things that you are teaching your daughters come from a flawed outlook on life. This way of thinking was not created by you but was adopted into your thinking through messages placed in front of you when you were young, your parents allowed you to be influenced by them because they were influenced by them also, but the only way to change what will inevitably happen to our people is to admit to your failures right now and seek a better way of raising our kids. Your failures are not just yours, we all share in them but as long as you believe that you have not done anything wrong in the upbringing of the Black children of today and admit to your part, we will never heal our wounded relationships between each other and then we are lost.

The Rise of the Video Vixen

The video vixen or what some have come to know as the video hoe started at the beginning of the video era. At first it was mostly white women strutting their stuff in front of the camera even when it was a Black band or group's song and trying to be sexually provocative.

Then in 1990 one of the first videos that featured sexually provocative Black women came by the way of The 2 Live Crew in Me So Horny. The women were wearing tight dresses, swim suits, biker shorts and lingerie, which in 1990 were staples of the Black community but had never been displayed on a medium that could reach the masses. The women in these videos would be looked upon as conservative by today's standards. 2 Live Crew had shocked the world in 1989 with their album cover for "As Nasty As They Wanna Be" featuring 4 Black women standing on the beach with their backs to the camera wearing thong bikinis with each member of the group positioned between the women's legs. Although Ice T had done something similar the year before, but his image of the thong bikini clad Black woman was on the inside of the album cover as opposed to the front. This was shocking to say the least and it drew the attention of the media thus thrusting 2 Live Crew into the national spotlight.

Although sexual lyrics were a part of a lot of rap songs and albums before this album it was the first to get national coverage for its contents and this in turn made more rebellious youths want to go out and get the album, which in turn increased album sales, and this is how the era of sexual hip hop began. Too Short had been rapping like this for years but it's because of this album that it gained a national audience and started to make album sells sky rocket. Along with the sky rocket in sells came more emcee's trying to repeat what 2 Live Crew had done. Then in 1990 the video for Me So Horny debuted and the era of the video vixen was born.

Until this point there were women in videos but after this video the women began to lose more clothes and dance more provocatively. In the following years we would start to see videos like "Rump Shaker" by Wreckx-N-Effect and Sir Mix-A-Lot's, "My Baby Got Back" start to grace the screen. These videos help to catapult these artist into the national spotlight and increase album sells for the artist just as it did for 2 Live Crew and from that point on the video vixen was a staple of the hip hop video.

At the beginning of this era there were two cable channels dedicated to music videos, BET (Black Entertainment Television) and MTV (Music TV). These channels quickly became part of the marketing strategy of music industry CEO's across the nation. The video was quickly becoming a great way to showcase your artist and because sex sales as they had recently witnessed, every video from a rapper had to feature scantily clad women who were dancing around the artist and in the background. The song didn't even have to be about partying or women period, it could be about killing people and there they were, just as pretty as can be, half naked women gyrating for the camera.

Now that every video had to feature video vixens a new industry was born which saw the likes of thousands of beautiful Black women being "objectified, degraded or demeaned" by what they were doing in the videos. Naturally this gave rise to protest by women, which in turn garnered the new industry more attention and a lot of young Black women around the nation started to feel like they looked just as good as or better than the women in these videos. And because a lot of Black women up to this point had low self esteem and did not look at Black as beautiful this new industry seemed to be an equalization of the playing fields. White women were always looked upon as sex symbols and only a few Black women were able to reach this plateau and those that did, did it through singing or as actresses. This new industry was now able to give Black women who could not sing or act a new way to showcase their beauty.

At the dawning of the video vixen era came the new industry of "Black beauty" which was a good thing. It created countless jobs for Black video directors, whom some of went on to direct movies. It created Black magazines focused on the underappreciated physique of the Black woman which then gave more Black women a chance to reach for the stars. Although few Black women that were featured in these videos ever went on to acting careers or as singers the industry has never suffered due to lack of willing vixens. Those who didn't achieve any substantial stardom outside of the industry, which is about 99% of them, were still able to make a living by doing appearances, magazines and creating websites which they used to showcase themselves.

The curse of the video vixen era is largely due to the coming of the Lil Kim Syndrome when the "use what you got to get what you want" mind state became the guiding factor for Black women in our neighborhoods. This attitude is akin to the "by any means necessary" attitude that Black men have. Although the words are from Malcolm X, a great man and Freedom fighter, the way Black youth use them is just about the complete opposite of how Malcolm used them. The problem with this new mind state was that far too many women were willing to do anything it took in the pursuit of fame and fortune.

Now that this new industry was booming, you started to see more women willing to be "degraded" to get paid up to $5000 for a video shoot. As more and more women became willing to do video shoots the competition to actually land the high paying coveted "main vixen" spot became harder and harder to secure by just being beautiful. At this point the men that were casting these videos started looking for women to do more than look good for the camera and thus the video hoe is born. When some of the Black women who were seeking to get in these videos found out that sexual favors could help them secure a job on a shoot, they started to initiate these favors in order to get a piece of the pie. They believed that they could parlay there video castings into a bigger, brighter career for themselves so they were willing to do just about anything to get into the game. When I say anything I mean anything, ask Karrine Steffans, the world's most notorious video vixen whom we will get to later.

These women were willing to have sex, oral, anal, or with another chick, whatever it took to get on set and be the "main girl". A lot of them were willing to do these things with people who were as low down the totem pole as members of the emcees entourage, which meant that she probably would have to end up doing something with the emcee, director, casting director or anyone else that she felt held the golden key to becoming the "main chick" in the video too. Now you have 100's of women lining up to try to get in a video and over half of them are willing to go the" extra mile" to get the spot.

There was a documentary done on this side of the industry on VH1 in 2005 entitled Hip Hop Videos: Sexploitation On The Set. It documented all the behind the scenes things that happen on the set and at casting calls. None of it was hearsay; it came from the mouths of some of leading women in the industry.

By the time this documentary had aired a new side of the industry had reared its ugly head in 2000 in the form of BET Uncut, a late night video show that aired any type of video imaginable as long as there was no nudity in them or the nude images were blurred. Uncut showcased rappers who didn't have the money to pay for high quality videos and top notch girls. It showcased the videos that can be done with a handheld video camera and any chick that was willing to make her butt jiggle in front of a camera. These women tended to be strippers and they were willing to do anything on camera which they demonstrated in the videos they were in.

The Exotic Dancer

The stripper for short, has been around since before hip hop and will be around until the end of time. Since the rise of videos as a medium for hip hop artist to get there songs listened to, strippers have been in on casting calls but never really got the lead roles as the main girl in videos until BET Uncut debuted. With this new video format they were able to get there moment in the sun along with other video vixens. They were willing to go the extra mile for far less than other mainstream video chicks because as strippers, they were already accustomed to exchanging sexual favors for small sums of money, not to say that every dancer will have sex with men for money, but a large percentage of them will do it, and that creates more competition within the exotic dancer community to get paid. If the dancer next to you is willing to go to the "Champaign Room" and you're not you're going to see a lot of money going into the pockets of your peers and not yours.

In the northern states being a dancer was considered taboo in the early 90's until around 1998 when Ice Cube made a movie titled "The Players Club". In the south the exotic dancer was not a job to ashamed of but a lot of women looked upon it as a career move or to get them through tough times and/or college. But after The Players Club women became more forward with their affiliation with exotic dancing.

Although the industry was big it became bigger due to more women sympathizing with the role of Diamond played by Lisa Raye, where she happened upon dancing while she was attending school due to the need to make some quick money. And she was a single mother with a dead beat dad as the child's father. As the movie showed there were lifelong dancers who were there just for the quick buck also, but for whatever reason the ranks of the exotic dancer increased after this movie.

2 Live Crew were the first musicians to make music directly aimed at the exotic dancer industry in the early 90's and Luke one of the members championed their cause throughout his career. He had faded into obscurity somewhat, although he was still touring the country doing Luke's Peep Show with strippers performing his hot mid 90's single Doo Doo Brown, which was a song that had women the country over trying to "pop that pussy" like strippers were able to do. Then Lil John came along in 97 and stole Luke's style of emceeing. By 2001 he was a national act and music that was initially targeted for strip clubs, so that the women could pop their butts and dance around on stage, would once again become a part of mainstream hip hop.

So as we see circa 98, strippers were starting to get national attention through movies and hip hop music, then approximately 2 years later, they got a new chance to realize their dreams of stardom with Uncut. Although it came on a 3:00 am in the morning just about every man that watched videos made sure that they caught as many episodes of it as they could.

Now that strippers were starting to get some shine on TV the industry began to grow even more in the background. They had a new medium for their services and it was being broadcast every night on cable. Once again you could see how young women were influenced by what they saw and figured that they could get paid also. The Lil Kim Syndrome was in full force and more and more Black women were thinking with this mentality.

As the industry grew in the background and BET Uncut became more popular mainstream hip hop artist started making videos strictly targeting the Uncut crowd. In 2003 Nelly produced a video called Tip Drill on his remix album that quickly became the number 1 talked about video on the streets and in every barbershop in the nation. It spawned numerous bootlegs and due to the frenzy other mainstream artist began to make Uncut videos to try to top his. Nelly had taken some of the top strippers and produced a high quality video which he then aired. After that 50 Cent, Snoop Dogg, Ludacris, and a host of others followed suit. Once again the exotic dancer was getting in on the video vixen craze and this time it started to pay off because a few of the girls from Nelly's video were able to spin there Uncut fame into websites and placements in other more main stream videos. At this time the internet vixen was starting to rise to claim her spot in the ever booming industry of new found "Black Beauty".

Circa 2002 - 2003 publications like Black Men, Smooth and King Magazine were being launched to showcase the women of this new industry also but the internet was and still is the driving force of this industry since its adoption by Black communities. As of 2008 80% of Blacks in this country has some form of access to the internet and 66% have broadband access. These magazines helped to spotlight otherwise over looked women who had been trying to tell the world that they were beautiful also and because so many of them felt disenfranchised and overlooked you started to see more and more women utilizing the internet as there medium to reach for the stars and alert the world that Black was beautiful. And now that strippers are starting to appear on the covers of Black magazines and in mainstream videos a new way to get paid was making its rise via the internet.

The Internet & Black Girls Gone Wild

With the proliferation of the internet in Black homes came more women trying to showcase themselves because they were being looked over by video producers and by the 3 major publications that served as the gateway for Black women to become household names and maybe one day become a main stream star.

In the beginning there were a few sites here and there but around 2003 the numbers started to rise because video vixens were then being seen out and about wearing luxury items and driving fancy cars. In interviews they were talking about their websites and how much money they were making from subscribers and for appearance fees which to the Black women who had adopted the Lil Kim Syndrome seemed to be their pot of gold. The internet vixen boom produced thousands of Melyssa Ford, Buffie The Body, Vida Guerra and Esther Baxter wannabe's. And when I say 1000's I mean 1000's. Every Black woman that thought she looked good or had a banging body was trying to become the next big internet sensation.

Because the internet was an easy way to scout for new talent the Black magazines started finding talent online and this lead to even more women throwing their hats into the ring. Once again the same formula took place. Black women in search for stardom find a new way to facilitate their dreams which in turn brings about more women trying to utilize these new means and only a few actually make it to the promised land, the video or into the pages of one of the Black magazines. By the time the internet craze was hitting full throttle the overall mission of becoming a main stream celebrity or star had taken a back seat to reaching for the cover of one of these magazines or just becoming the "main vixen" in a video. The new initiates into the industry knew that their chances of reaching stardom outside of the Black beauty industry was a shot in the dark because few women who tried to utilize these means were able to move beyond them, and some of the ones that did were not Black, ethnic, but not Black.

This led to the new internet vixen having to; once again, do a little bit more than just pose for a camera to get subscribers to their sites. Now they would have to be fully nude within the pages to attract the dollars of voyeurs. These new women who knew that they could make a pretty nice amount of money from their internet sites, whose idols were Lil Kim and Trina, and now Melyssa Ford Buffie The Body and Vida Guerra were using what they had to get what they wanted. And what they want is money, because money brings security and a semblance of happiness. Because most people think that the more things you have the happier you will be, and everything that these women were doing was for that reason.

The Mirror Model

The internet has spawned an even uglier monster in the name of Black beauty and it's the amateur porn star and mirror model. I will talk about the amateur porn star a little later but for now the mirror model will be discussed. All you need is a digital camera, webcam or phone cam, and a mirror and now all kinds of nude and semi nude pictures are being posted all over the web.

For the past five years or so anyone with a couple of pictures has been calling themselves a model. All kinds of services have popped up on the internet for this amateur group of women to showcase themselves if they don't have enough money to pay for professional pictures and get their own website. These sites literally have 10's of thousands of members trying to become the next big model in this industry, not just Black women, but this book is about Black women so that's who I'm focusing on. The vast majority, say 99% of these women are not getting paid one dime for the pictures that you see on the internet, semi nude or nude, not one dime. They are all doing it with the hopes of being discovered by someone that can rescue them from their abysmal existence. In 2010 we have 100's of thousands of women on Myspace, Facebook, and other social media platforms half naked poking their butts out claiming they are models although they are not getting paid to model.

And Youtube and the rest of these sites have created the nightmare of every father on planet, to keep his daughter off the pole. No father wants to see his baby girl stripping yet 10's of thousands of girls that get younger and younger as you go are on these sights doing every move that they see strippers on these sights do. All one has to do is search for booty popping and you could spend days sifting through the videos of Black women shaking what their mother gave them to the tunes of your favorite artist. These women are not even getting paid for this and probably will never get paid for it unless they graduate to exotic dancer because that's about the only industry that's looking for the talents that they are displaying.

And Along Came Superhead
(The Karrine Steffans Phenomenon)

While the internet was kicking into high gear a young video vixen was staking *her* claim in the industry. Karrine "Superhead" Steffans as she was once called came into the video scene in Jay Z's video "Big Pimpin" around 2000. She had been the girlfriend of a hip hop star previously and had a baby by him. Their relationship was rocky and she eventually became his ex, but because she knew some people in the industry she was able to parlay her connects into a brief career as a video vixen. I believe she only did about 3 videos or so before she decided that going to casting calls and such was not what she was best suited for. At the age of 21 she was now a video vixen but because she was a product of the Lil Kim Syndrome of the early to mid 90's she decided that she had something that rappers wanted, and that was sex. She was a beautiful young woman with a nice body and wasn't afraid to use her attributes to get her to the riches she so desired. After a brief stint as a vixen she decided to become an all out hip hop prostitute or escort to put it mildly. This is how she was dubbed Superhead. Because of her ability to make a man ejaculate with her mouth in record time she had become the talk of the industry. She wore the badge proudly and quickly became the go to girl in the industry for sexual pleasures.

This garnered her all kinds of lavish gifts, 10's of thousands of dollars from some of her acquaintances, paid for apartments and cars, she was living the life. Guys in the industry who were either married or had girlfriends would pay her handsomely to keep her mouth shut once she left their hotel rooms, and it was all good until she had been passed around enough and they stopped contacting her. Immediately she was confronted with a lavish lifestyle with no way to pay for it. As she has been quoted saying in numerous interviews, she would call on guys who had once given her 1000's of dollars for a night with her and they wouldn't even answer their phones. She had been cut off in her time of need, no one cared anymore and she was faced with homelessness with her child.

So faced with these impending problems she took matters into her own hands and got a 3 book publishing deal to reveal all the secrets that she had concerning her sexual exploits with hip hop, r & b, and athletic stars. It was worth $7.5 million and her first book Confessions of a Video Vixen instantly became a NY Times best seller upon release in 2005. She had successfully used what she had to get what she wanted and now she was a millionaire. Since that book she has published 2 others and has become one of the top known Black women in America.

After seeing her success countless other women tried to imitate what she did but none have been able to do what she did. Even a gay guy tried to "out" Black closeted gay's to no avail. The latest to try is an internet chick that goes by the name of Kat Stacks but she was quickly dusted under the rug and what she thought was going to be her ticket to fame has become a laughing point for people perusing internet video sites.

Although no one else has achieved Karrine's level of fame for doing this one can know that there are millions of dollars that are being exchanged from hand to hand quietly to keep information like this out of tabloids and off the internet. We need only look at the recent outing of Tiger Woods to know that men are still paying and women are still being paid.

The Porn Star

Porno has been around for as long as movies have been around but Black women in porno relatively new compared to white women in porn. Back in the days you would have few women here and there but not like it is today. Due to the internet and the AVN awards porno has become a part of every household in the world. It was always a booming industry but because of the internet people don't have to leave their homes to get their fix, all they need to do is type boobs or ass in a search engine and viola it's right there.

Black porn has steadily risen over the decades due to the coming of the Lil Kim Syndrome and the irrational thought that Black men would rather be with white women instead of Black women. The reason why so many men would look at white girls in Playboy and Penthouse was because they rarely had Black women in them. The same goes for porno movies, but as more Black women started to become porn stars Black men started to watch them more, as demonstrated today.

The Black porn star actually got her first glimpse by the mainstream audience in the Tupac video, "However You Want it" around 1996, which featured Heather Hunter and Angel Kelly, two of the first Black porn stars to cross over to mainstream white porn. Heather Hunter retired and tried to become a rapper later on but never saw any mainstream fame. Her album came out in 2005 which was when Black porn was booming and the sexual promiscuity of Black women was on display for the world to see. Her timing was right but her skills weren't there so she never became big in hip hop.

After Lil Kim came into existence and the" use what you got to get what you want attitude" became the driving force in Black women you can see the steady rise of Black women in porn. More and more women who were disenfranchised and searching for fame and stardom began to shun the new conventional female emcee or vixen model and follow the Heather hunter model. Men were willing to pay them 1000's of dollars to have sex with them on film, so of course you had some takers, nothing like the vixens and exotic dancer boom but more Black women were willing so more Black women were now being featured in porn videos. At this same time the young Black women who couldn't make it as rappers or video vixens were becoming strippers and internet models so in order to make some money some of them decided to give porn a try and so goes the story.

At a time when Black women were still trying to find their paths porn was becoming more and more a part of mainstream society and less and less taboo. With the AVN Awards, the porno industries equivalent of the Oscars, Black women who were already willing to sell sex or just plain old give it away to achieve money and stardom started to see new opportunities in the porn industry. They were doing it anyway, so the next progression was to sell it on film. As regular pimpin and whoring was dying, internet pimpin and porn pimps were on the rise. It isn't illegal therefore why not try it. More and more Black women who saw it as an ends to means started to indulge in the industry, even Karrine Steffans tried it and did a couple of scenes before she wrote her book.

Now in 2010 if you do a search for Black porno you will find 10's of thousands of clips of Black women doing everything under sun sexually. You'll see a lot of the same women in clips, but if you search you start to realize that there are literally 10's of thousands of different women in these clips. There is no shortage of them across the internet.

What's really disturbing is the 10's of thousands of amateur porno videos that are on display online. The vast majority of these Black women are not getting paid one dime for their videos. A large percentage of the clips are from camera phones which means that the guy she is having sex with or giving oral sex is then going home and uploading these videos to the internet. This free porn boom has spawned numerous sights to accommodate the millions of clips that are on the internet.

Are these audition tapes so that these beautiful Black women can show what they can do, so they can someday make it into the world of porn or are they just a symptom of the times? Either way something has to be done to slow it down and eventually end it. Too many of our Black Queens are falling victim to this type of non-sense. How many men do you think are going to want to marry you when they can do an internet search and find you naked all over the place or doing amateur porn for free? That is not how Queens behave, but yet and still you want us to call you Queens and treat you as such. In the world I live in we call women like that whores and most men are not going to marry whores, period.

As you can see, hip hop has had a very large role in the state of the Black female in the 21st century and it is directly because of it that certain thought patterns are prevalent in the Black women of today. I am not trying say that the "use what you got to get what you want attitude" or what I call The Lil Kim Syndrome just came into being during the 90's. What I'm saying here is that after the rise of Lil Kim this attitude became the dominant attitude in Black women. This in no way says that every woman who listened to Lil Kim became a version of her, but she did usher in an unmistakable thought pattern for the Black women of our time. In the mid 90's when she rose to fame, Black women were looking for a champion of their cause and Lil Kim embodied the spirit of do it yourself and do it by whatever means you see fit. This manifested itself in absentee mother and/or fatherless daughters as the women who started to become exotic dancers, porn stars and internet prostitutes that we see today that are trying to sell their bodies to achieve the American dream.

Reality TV and the Nationalization of Black Female Stereotypes

The rise of the reality star over the past 10 years has help to foster some of the unwanted attitudes of The Lil Kim Syndrome generation. All over TV the argumentative, caddy, and angry Black woman is being displayed so that the world can see. There are plenty of Black women on regular shows like comedies and dramas on TV also. These women are being portrayed in a positive light and they exude independence and strength. They take care of their children and other responsibilities like the vast majority of Black women do in real life.

As for the reality star, there is an entirely different formula that's being used. The producer for these shows are looking for wild, uncouth, loud mouthed, the overall tactless Black women. The more outlandish she is the longer she lasts on a show.

This formula was first put into effect on Flavor of Love a VH1 hit that pitted 15 – 20 women against each other to win the love of Flavor Flav, a hip hop legend and new reality TV star. His show consisted of a lot of very outspoken Black women who would argue, throw drinks on each other and almost come to physical blows on just about every episode.

One of the contestants that lasted the longest was a lady by the name of New York. She made it to the end but lost out to the better looking Hoopz. But because of her willingness to be the stereotypical ghetto chick she was able to come back on the show the next season and make it to the end again, at which point she lost again. The ratings with her on the show were always very high so VH1 gave her a contract to do her own show, but this time men would be competing for her. Her show debuted with high ratings and once again the stereotypical ghetto attitude had found its place on TV, now it would be rooted in reality TV.

Now that Black women were seeing the new formula for success it would not take long to see women popping up on these shows trying to imitate New York in an effort to duplicate her success. Luckily the dating show formula simmered down and no one has been able to duplicate the fame of Flavor of Love, but it spawned shows like Rock of Love, I Love New York, Real Chance of Love and For the Love of Ray J.

All these shows used the same formula and had a little success and the ratings were always higher when the girls were having cat fights, so the cat fight became the new draw for these shows. They make sure that there's plenty of alcohol on set to keep the women inebriated and they make sure that there's always a few women that hate each other.

So with this formula at hand the Black version of Real Housewives debuted in Atlanta. The Real Housewives show was supposed to be based on friends who were married and their day to day comings and goings like the original series in Orange County. But the Atlanta spin off was a bit different. One of the women wasn't even married (the white one) and one of them was going through a nasty divorce, and was painting her soon to be ex-husband in an unfavorable light.

A show that originally aired as a show for rich socialite white women was now showcasing Black women, but the formula was a bit different. The Black women weren't as well off except two of them, an ex-NBA and an ex-NFL player's wife.

After the first season they dropped the ex-NBA player's wife and brought on a new woman who wasn't married but was "engaged", because she didn't really bring any drama to the show and the more drama the hire ratings.

During the second season you could see that the formula for success for the Atlanta spinoff was shaping up the same way as the other Black reality shows. The other drama free cast member who was married to the ex-NFL player saw her face time diminish during season 2, which lead to her being let go and them bringing on 2 new girls for season 3. As this was written before the launch of season 3 I can't tell you what happened but I can tell you what is in store during the 3rd season based on the bios on the web page for this series.

Season 3 will see a married stable relationship dropped from the show and they will pick up two new "wives". One of the new women is married and is an accomplished attorney but she has drama because her younger husband went to jail for a white collar crime and they're trying to have a baby and get through the BS. The second new "wife" isn't married but engaged and really doesn't want to be married as it states in her bio, so her drama is her fiancé has given her an ultimatum which she now has to ponder on during the season.

So in the course of 2 seasons as the third season is yet to air this show has went from 3 cast members that are married, one getting a divorce and one dating a married man. To 2 married, one rumored to be going through a divorce, one going through drama because her husband is a white collar criminal, 3 single, one dating a married man, one playing the field, one who's fiancé was murdered during season 2 and 1 engaged to be married that doesn't want to be married.

It seems as if the producers think that the ratings will be higher if there's more arguing and cat fighting going on even if it's supposed to be about the everyday things "wives" do. Can we blame them for it, when ratings do skyrocket when Black women are on TV acting a fool?

The latest installment to the Black female reality TV circle is The Basketball Wives, which only had 1 married lady on the show. The producer, Shaunie O'neal, had just gone through a divorce with her high profile husband Shaquille right before the show aired and she was only on one show. The rest of the shows she was doing commentary but she was never seen out and about with the girls.

There were six cast members and one was married but they named the show "Basketball Wives". One of the ladies was engaged, one was an ex-cheerleader who had a baby by one of the top basketball players in Orlando, one used to be "engaged" and had a kid by a player, one had two kids by a player and who knows if she was ever engaged and one was married but going through tough times with her husband, which seemed as if it was going to end in divorce.

Some of the advice she was getting from these other ladies was to cheat on him because he did it to her. Three of the unmarried bitter basketball groupies, excluding Shaunie and the one that was engaged, were telling the only one that was married to cheat on her husband on camera. Then they all even the married one, excluding Shaunie again, were trying to discourage the one that was engaged from getting married. The show consisted of the basketball groupies going to industry parties and arguing with other groupies about who was sleeping with whose baller.

I still don't' understand how they got away with calling it "Basketball Wives when only one of the women was married. The ratings must have been good enough for the network because there's a season two set to air on VH1.

So now that we see the formula, ask yourself why this formula? Is this what Black women have become? How did it come to this and who directly benefits from it being this way?

Take a look around you and you'll see that this formula does not paint the Black woman in a good light, nor does it help to prop up Black on Black relationships and/or family. What it does is give women who are already bitter for one reason or another, new ammo for their attitudes. If you are a child of the Lil Kim Syndrome then you will see these women as somewhat heroic because they were able to get themselves in a better position in life and all they had to do was "use what they had to get what they wanted".

These women on this show were a direct product of this attitude and you can see it in the way they act. It's all about how they look and if they can find an athlete that will take care of them. Most of them have been with numerous athletes until they were able to find one that wanted to "wife" them or at least have a baby by them so that they can get that child support payment for the next 18 years.

Baller Alert
(When Being a Groupie Becomes Option # 1)

The groupie has been around since the beginning of stardom. At the dawning of radio, when a man's voice became recognizable by the masses women were fawning over them. When movies were created and were mass marketed the male stars became the most sought after men on the planet. Women saw them as sexier, more masculine and more financially stable than an average man, and this created 10's of thousands of fans and 1000's of women who were willing to have sex with these men for a chance at their lifestyles.

The groupie mentality is a combination of things. 1) The thought that men who are entertainers or athletes are better looking than the average person, 2) That they have money and are willing to spend it on their women, 3) That being with one of them will bring security, 4) The thought that the entertainer or athlete will choose them over the other women that they sleep with, and 5) The "use what you have to get what you want attitude".

As professional athletics became a part of the American fabric the same phenomenon occurred with them. The ones who were the most recognizable became sex symbols and more and more women became willing sexual conquests for them.

During the 50's and 60's Black men started to be recruited into the ranks of the American professional athlete. This was when the Black groupie started to come into the picture. Over the first couple decades of the Black athlete the Black groupie was a small segment of the landscape but as more and more Black men became athletes Black groupie began to increase in numbers.

At the same time the Black athlete was growing in numbers Black entertainers were also growing in numbers which gave the Black woman with a groupie mentality more ways to pursue her piece of the American dream.

In the 70's during the Blaxploitation era and leading into the dead beat dad era Wilt Chamberlain was using his stardom to have sex with what he says was over 20,000 women. Some people dispute his claims but by looking at the climate today surrounding Black athletes and groupies I can see how it was possible. With fewer athletes to choose from he would have been a very, very hot commodity.

As Black women were being abandoned and some pushing their men away to be with other men or to receive Welfare, the "use what you have to get what you want" attitude was starting to be taught to young Black women across the nation by their angry and misguided mothers.

This resulted in Black women in high school choosing the athlete over the regular guy because the athlete might make it to the pros and then she would be able to share in his riches. The same concept was being repeated throughout high schools and colleges across the nation. This in turn led to more Black men wanting to become athletes and entertainers.

During the 80's and 90's the ranks of the Black athlete and entertainer grew tremendously and along with it came more and more women that were willing to fit the groupie mold so they could be taken care of by these men. During this time Hip Hop was taking root and helping to perpetuate stereotypical Black male and female behavior. And now that Hip Hop artist were starting to be seen as high net worth entertainers, the groupie moved into the Hip Hop realm also. That move created the Video Vixen and Lil Kim, who went on to make the "use what you have to get what you want" attitude the prevalent thought pattern for disenfranchised Black women across the nation.

At the time that the Black athlete and entertainer were becoming more and more part of the American landscape an industry of voyeurism was becoming part of pop culture also. This industry started to highlight athletes and entertainers more which helped to create more groupies who wanted to be seen out and about with these guys. Then these publications started to report on the amount of children that they had, which should have been a red light for potential groupies, but to the contrary it became an open invitation to Black women who now wanted to get next to athletes and entertainers so that they could get pregnant and have their children. This would give them 18 years of security via the child support system if the star didn't want to marry them. After Lil Kim this phenomenon grew like wild fire, women were adopting the Lil Kim Syndrome and trying to get pregnant by any and every star they could.

During the past 15 years the groupie has gone from just going after nationally recognized athletes and entertainers to Black women who go after drug dealers, anyone associated with a star, and any star that has any type of recognizable name.

Over the past 10 years message boards dedicated to groupies and their pursuit of what they call Baller's have sprung up to help would be groupies navigate the treacherous field of landing a baller who will spend lavishly on her, and if she can get pregnant by him she's set for life.

As reality TV has become a mainstay in American culture we now see TV shows that highlight the groupie. From Keeping up With the Kardashians to The Basketball Wives, these shows are giving young Black women across America a look into the "fabulous" world of what being a groupie can get them.

The one thing that they should take from these shows is that, even though some of them will get some money and some notoriety for being a groupie the vast majority of them will only come away from the encounter with little more than a notch on their un-chastity belt.

From Now to Forever

After reading what I've written in this book some women will undoubtedly label me as a Black woman basher, but rest assured that I am far from that. I want you all to know that I love Black women and the only reason that I decided to tackle this problem is because it needs to be done in order to start the healing process amongst Black men and women in order to save the Black family. Some Black women have adopted attitudes that are not conducive to them being in sustainable relationships and getting married, yet they believe that they are not at fault for their current condition in any way, shape or form.

As Black women are searching for answers to their relationship problems with Black men I wanted to show you where you went wrong and why these things need to be fixed or we will continue to march down the same road to nowhere.

Black men are far more conservative when it comes down to the women that they consider to be suitable as a wife than what is portrayed in the various forms of media that showcase Black male thought. This is where the problems come from. Since the rise of NWA, Too Short, 2 Live Crew and various other Hip Hop artist that promoted a misogynistic message of sexual promiscuity and demeaning attitude toward Black women, Black women have been trying to live up to these standards and have become what these lyrics rapped about.

In these lyrics Black men have basically represented the Black female as a sex toy and too many Black women have become just that, but if you look at the wives of these same men that have perpetuated this myth you will see the exact opposite. They always keep their wives out of the limelight and away from the cameras, except for Ice T, but we all know that he has a pseudo-pimp label to live up to. No matter what they say in their lyrics or try to push off to the world as who they are and what they want their women to do, their wives never fit that profile. So in short, black women have been trying to live up to figment of some ones imagination. The women that they rhyme about are not the women that they are going to marry. Yeah, they will have sex with these ladies but that's about it, but the one that they call there wife will usually be almost the complete opposite of these women. This goes for sports stars and entertainers also. If they break up with their long time women or get divorced then you might see them with the scantily clad video vixen groupie type but how many of them actually marry this chick, that's the question that really needs to be asked.

My question to Black women reading this is, do you all want to have stable sustainable relationships and get married or are you ok with the way things are unfolding within the ranks of Black women in America? If you want these things but have not been able to find them then you will have to look deep within yourselves to find what's wrong with you and your thinking. It may be you and the way that you think, or it might not be but at least you will know what to look for after reading "The Pawn Queen".

THE SIMPLEST SOLUTION FOR THE PROBLEMS AT HAND IS CHANGE THE WAY THAT YOU THINK AND YOU CAN CHANGE YOUR WORLD.

In my next book Philosophical Street Chronic (The Making of the 21st Century Black Male) I will dig deep into the psyche of the young Black male and attempt to show where we went wrong also. And that we have caused more damage than we care to admit through Hip Hop and the way we have treated Black women during my generation. Black men will have to look deep within themselves in order to rectify our erroneous thinking also, so that we can stop the problems that exist today and fix them at the source.

The Conclusion

I wrote this book because I came to the realization that Black women were searching for answers and the ones that they were getting were not changing the way that they think. As an advocate for the change the way you think and you can change your world philosophy I realized that Black women were subject to the same type of brainwashing that Black men were subject to but their programming was different. They were being programmed to think a certain way so that they could aid in the systematic destruction of the Black male and family.

This was a profound thought because it was so far outside of what the status quo Black philosophical community was used to hearing, let alone writing about. Up to the point that I decided to write this, I had never heard or read anything about how the Black woman was being conditioned in various ways to think and react a certain way for the purpose of bringing about the demise of the Black family and man. Every study and/or philosophical lecture up to this point was about the Black male and how we are destroying ourselves. Not one about how Black women have aided in this destruction

Maybe it's because the people who have been doing the writing up to now were pre-occupied with themselves and their careers or maybe it's because they just didn't know, but for whatever reason it may be, it has not been the topic of discussion.

While writing another book my wife would tell me about the things that she had seen posted on Black message boards concerning Black women, it dawned on me that the conditioning of Black women go far beyond the issue of skin tone and hair quality but it permeates deep into their psyche also, and it is manifesting itself in various ways.

I know that the things described in this book will not fall on deaf ears and the women and men that read this book will come to an agreement that we as a people need to come to a real understanding that we are both at fault for the situation that we see in Black communities today. As long as black women see no fault in themselves we will never heal and become what we once were.

THIS IS WHY THIS BOOK IS NEEDED!

As slaves you were conditioned to believe that the Black man could not protect you or provide for you as the white man could. You imbedded it into the way that you thought about the Black man, but we endured.

During the Jim Crow Era you were conditioned to believe that Black men wanted white women and light skinned "good hair" women and we endured.

We stood beside each other and continued to forge a path for Black people to shine our greatness on humanity into the Civil Rights Era and after they assassinated our Black leaders, we endured.

We have been through dead beat dads, crack and AIDS but still we endure.

The latest test for the endurance of the Black family has been placed in front of us in the 80's and we are still here. We have weathered every storm and everything that has been placed in our paths we have overcome and still have risen as a people.

Do you want this to be our demise, do you want us to fade back into obscurity and become third or fourth class citizens

The choice is yours, all you have to do is understand that the path that we are headed down as a people holds no future unless we come to the understanding that we are the Alpha and the Omega and that your destiny is our destiny. You cannot think that your actions have no relevancy on our destiny; you cannot believe that you have done no wrong and expect us to heal.

Over the last 40 plus years of our existence in America the Black man has lost his way and so has the Black woman.

After the death of MLK a shift has occurred and we have been headed in direction of self fulfillment. The Black leaders who were supposed to pick up the ball and run with it after MLK's assassination decided to become opportunist because they were not willing to die for the cause. The ones that were willing to die met their demise at the end of a bullet, Hoover made sure of that and since then we have been wandering in the wilderness searching for ourselves trying to make something out of our existence.

This is but the first step toward the healing process.

Once again, we are all in the same boat, let's stop fighting with one another and row in unison. We are all trying to reach the same destination. I have your back, I hope you have mine.

Coming in 2011

Philosophical Street Chronic

(The Making of the 21st Century Black Male)

40 Years in the Wilderness

(The Making of the 21st Century Black Family)

Visit us at woulardmediadistribution.com

www.ingramcontent.com/pod-product-compliance
Lightning Source LLC
Chambersburg PA
CBHW051710040426
42446CB00008B/805